PRONOUNCING
FRENCH

PRONOUNCING FRENCH
A Guide for Students

Jean-Michel Picard
Vera Regan

University College Dublin Press
Preas Choláiste Ollscoile Bhaile Átha Cliath

First published 2001 by University College Dublin Press,
Newman House, 86 St Stephen's Green, Dublin 2, Ireland
www.ucdpress.ie

ISBN 1 900621 64 9

Cataloguing in Publication data available from the British Library

Typeset in Ireland in Photina and Gill Sans
by Elaine Shiels, Bantry, Co. Cork
Printed in Ireland by Betaprint, Dublin

Contents

Acknowledgements

The authors wish to express their thanks to
Dr Maeve Conrick and Dr Robert Crawshaw for
their helpful comments. They would also like to
thank Barbara Mennell for her encouragement
and careful editing.

INTRODUCTION

Learning a language is learning to communicate. Efficient communication supposes not only a good knowledge of vocabulary and grammar, but also good pronunciation.

Why is pronunciation important?

You may already have noticed that it is sometimes difficult to understand foreigners who are quite fluent in English, but fail to convey what they mean because their accent is too 'foreign' and you do not recognise words which are familiar to you. The same applies to all languages. You may have to communicate with French people holidaying or working in Ireland or Britain, or want to have a discussion with local people when you travel in France and, unless they recognise the sounds of their own language, they will find it quite difficult to understand you.

Accurate pronunciation is essential. Mistakes in pronunciation can lead to loss of meaning or misunderstanding. For example if you confuse [p] and [b] and ask for a crate of *pierre* instead of *bière*, you may go thirsty for a while until the misunderstanding is cleared up. Such mistakes in pronunciation affect the meaning of the sentence and will require your immediate attention. Other defects in pronunciation do not change the meaning of words but contribute to an impression of 'foreign accent', which some might find charming while it may irritate others. For example, if an English speaker pronounces *passe* [pɑs] like *pass* [pɑ:s], thus producing a long vowel instead of a short one, their French listeners will probably understand, but will immediately notice that the first language of the speaker is English.

In the process of acquiring correct pronunciation, the first task is to recognise and correctly identify the sounds of the French language. They are different in many ways from the sounds of English and becoming conscious of the differences is the first necessary step.

What are the main differences between French and English?

From a phonetic viewpoint, French is a 'tense' language as opposed to English which is 'lax'. Production of French sounds requires a greater effort of articulation, involving facial muscles, and tenseness of the larynx and vocal cords. Also, French people give the impression of constantly moving their lips and using incredible energy when they speak. For example when French people hesitate, they say 'euh', with their lips clearly rounded. An English speaker would rather say 'eh', with his/her lips in a neutral position. That impression is correct, and speaking French requires a greater effort of articulation than English. You should get used to that idea and start exercising all your facial muscles. There is an element of acting in learning French: don't be shy.

French is also more 'frontal' than English. It means that the sounds tend to be produced more towards the front of the mouth. For example, French [t] is pronounced with the tongue touching the teeth (dental position) while English [t] is pronounced with the tongue reaching only behind the teeth-ridge (alveolar position).

Another characteristic of French is vowel anticipation. This means that in each syllable the vowel is the dominant sound and influences the pronunciation of the preceding consonant. For example, in the syllable [ti], the vowel [i] is pronounced with fully spread lips and the spreading of the lips affects the entire syllable. On the other hand, if the central vowel is rounded, the whole syllable will be rounded as in *tout* [tu]. The exact opposite exists in English where the consonant influences the pronunciation of the preceding vowel as in *man* [mæn], where the final consonant influences the vowel *a* which becomes nasalised.

Finally, diphthongisation, that is the formation of a vowel combining two vocalic sounds, is a characteristic of English, which is rarely found in French. For example, the sound of the French word *dé* [de] is very different from English *day* [deɪ], which is pronounced with a diphthong. In this respect Irish students find it easier to produce true French vowels since English spoken in Ireland is less diphthongised than standard English.

The speech organs

Speech is a complex process which involves several organs of the human body. These are:

1. **The lungs**
    When we speak, the air comes from the lungs through the windpipe and is released through the nose and mouth.

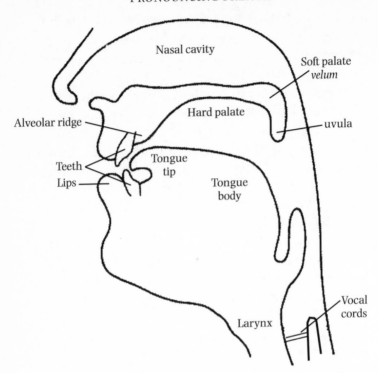

2. The vocal cords

These are two horizontal membranes set inside the throat (larynx) which can be controlled to stop the air from leaving the lungs (glottal stop), to allow the air to escape freely (voiceless sounds) or to vibrate (voiced sounds). If you put your hand against your throat while saying [d], [g], or [z], you will feel your vocal cords vibrating inside your throat. The sound produced when they vibrate is called 'voicing'. [b], [d], [g], [v] and [z] are voiced consonants while [p], [t], [k], [f] and [s] are called voiceless since they are produced without vibration of the vocal cords.

4

3. **The uvula**

   This is the small fleshy part which hangs down
   at the back of your mouth from your palate. It can
   vibrate, for example when you gargle, or when you
   pronounce one type of French r called 'uvular' or
   'rolled' [ʀ].

4. **The nose**

   As well as through the mouth, air can be expelled
   through the nose. When you close your lips, air can
   escape only through the nose: this is what you do
   when you hum a tune. In English all vowels are
   produced by letting the air escape through the mouth:
   they are oral vowels. Your nose allows you to produce
   another type of vowel which is called a nasal vowel.
   The two sets of vowels exist in French. When you let
   the air escape freely through your mouth you produce
   oral vowels such as [ɑ], [ɔ], [ɛ] and [œ], but if you use
   the very same articulation and force the air mostly
   through your nose, you will produce the nasal vowels
   [ɑ̃], [ɔ̃], [ɛ̃], and [œ̃].

5. **The mouth**

   Inside the mouth we find

   (*a*) the alveolar ridge (behind the teeth)
   (*b*) the hard palate
   (*c*) the soft palate

   Depending on the position of the soft palate or the
   position of the tongue against the teeth ridge or the
   hard palate, different sounds are produced. The
   terms alveolar, post-alveolar, palatal, velar are used
   to describe these sounds.

6. **The lips**

    Lips are characterised by their mobility. They can
    be fully rounded or spread, with a wide range of
    positions in between. The movement of the lips is
    essential in the articulation of the French language.
    In general, while English speakers tend to keep their
    lips in a neutral position, French speakers alternate
    between the two extreme positions, fully spread or
    fully rounded, thus producing a strong contrast
    between the different vowels.

7. **The tongue**

    In the process of producing sounds, the tongue
    can be lowered or raised. Three main parts are set
    in action: the tip, the middle and the back of the
    tongue. When you pronounce [t] as in *ta tante*,
    the tip of your tongue touches the teeth ridge.
    When you pronounce [k] as in *qui* [ki], the middle
    of your tongue is in contact with the hard palate.
    When linguists use the terms 'high' (= 'close') or
    'low' (= 'open') vowels, they refer to the position
    of the tongue inside the mouth.

8. **The teeth**

    Sounds such as [t], [d], [f] and [v] are produced by
    contact between the teeth and the tongue or the lips.
    In order to pronounce [f] as in *fille*, you have to set
    your upper teeth against your lower lip.

Vowels and consonants

The sounds of a language are divided into two main
categories: vowels and consonants.

The difference between the two categories is whether the air is obstructed by the speech organs or not. When you produce a vowel, the air flows freely through the mouth and the nose. For example, when you pronounce [a], none of the speech organs restricts the production of the sound. On the contrary, in order to produce a consonant, the flow of air must be impeded at some point, for example by the lips (as in [b]), or by the tongue and the teeth (as in [t]). Obstruction may be total as in [p] or partial as in [s] (fricative) or in [l] (lateral).

As we have seen above, French vowels are divided into oral vowels and nasal vowels, as opposed to English where only oral vowels are encountered. The difference between the two is that oral vowels are produced with the flow of air going through the mouth while nasal vowels are produced by lowering the soft palate and letting the air flow partly through the nose. The French nasal vowels are: [ɑ̃], [ɔ̃], [ɛ̃], et [œ̃]. However, it should be pointed out that [œ̃], as in *un parfum*, is slowly disappearing in modern day French. Most French people tend to replace [œ̃] by [ɛ̃], as in *fin*. For example, *un jour* is pronounced /ɛ̃ʒuʀ/.

Vowels are defined
(*a*) by the opening of the lower jaw, which determines the relative height of the tongue. These positions have been classified in four categories: 'close', 'close-mid', 'open-mid' and 'open'. A 'close' vowel will be produced by raising the tongue towards the palate with the mouth being slightly opened, while an 'open' vowel will be produced by lowering your jaw and consequently your tongue.

(*b*) by the position of the tongue towards the front of the mouth or towards the back. This is the difference between 'front' and 'back' vowels. In between is the 'central' position.

(*c*) by the position of the lips, whether 'rounded' or 'spread'.

(*d*) by the manner in which the air is expelled, whether through the mouth (oral vowels) or through the nose (nasal vowels).

The vocalic sounds [i], [u] and [ɑ] exist in all languages because they are found in the most extreme points of all vocalic systems.

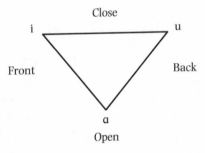

[i] and [u] are 'close' vowels. The tongue is raised and the lower jaw nearly closed. [a] is an 'open' vowel. The jaw is opened and the tongue is lowered. [i] and [u] are contrasted because, when [i] is pronounced, the tongue is placed towards the front of the mouth, while it is positioned towards the back of the mouth when [u] is articulated. [i] is a front vowel, as opposed to [u] which is a back vowel.

In between these extreme positions (close/open and front/back), several intermediary positions are possible. [e] and [o] are less close than [i] and [u] just as [ɛ] and [ɔ] are not as open as [a]. When we draw the diagram of the

8

French vowel system, we end up with a trapezium, which can be represented thus :

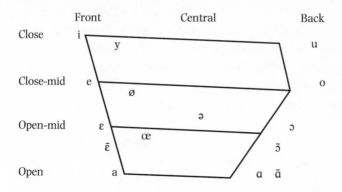

Trapezium of the French vowels

Unlike English vowels, French vowels keep their quality regardless of their position within the word. For example, in English, vowels in unstressed position tend to lose their vocalic identity and are reduced to sounds nearing the neutral [ə]. In French, the lips remain in the same position and muscular tenseness is maintained. For the second language learner, the advantage is that, once the proper articulation is achieved, there is no need to worry about possible variations linked to a stressed or unstressed position within the word. For example, if you pronounce the word 'confortable' in French, the vowels keep their original timbre /kɔ̃ fɔʀ tabl/, but in the English word 'comfortable' /kʌm fət əbl/, the vowels in the last two syllables have been reduced to [ə].

The International Phonetic Alphabet

Although alphabet was developed to record the spoken word in writing, most alphabetically written languages are unphonetic, mostly because spelling has remained static while the spoken language keeps evolving. For example the *k* in English *knee* is not pronounced any more but reflects an earlier stage of the language. There can be quite a difference between the way we write words and the way we pronounce them. At times, it may appear totally illogical. The same spelling can represent different sounds as in English *bough* /baʊ/, *cough* /kɒf/ and *through* /θruː/.

French is no exception and there are discrepancies between spellings and sounds. For example, different spellings may in fact represent the same sound as in *plein, faim, thym* and *matin*, which are all pronounced with the nasal sound [ɛ̃]. Very often, words contain letters which are not pronounced at all. For example, you do not pronounce *x* in *gateaux* /gato/. Also, there is no difference between *il chante* /ilʃɑ̃t/ and *ils chantent* /ilʃɑ̃t/. As you can see, there is no exact correspondence between spelling and pronunciation.

This is why linguists have created an alphabet which is nearer to pronunciation and represents sounds rather than morphology or grammatical markers. It is called the IPA alphabet because it was devised by the International Phonetic Association (IPA), established in Paris in 1886. For each sound there is a corresponding symbol. It is now used in all modern dictionaries as a guide to the pronunciation of individual words. Usually, the phonetic pronunciation is given at the beginning of each entry, immediately after the headword. It is a most useful tool for the second language learner as it allows us to find the correct pronunciation of new words we might encounter

10

in our reading without ever having heard them. Phonetic symbols of the IPA alphabet are written in square brackets (e.g. [ɛ], [ð], [ɔ]).

In the following table, you will find the lists of IPA phonetic symbols for French and English. Remember that, in spite of the similarity of symbols, the quality of sounds is different in the two languages.

IPA phonetic symbols

French		English		French		English	
VOWELS		VOWELS		CONSONANTS		CONSONANTS	
[ə]	le	[ə]	ago	[p]	pont	[p]	pen
[a]	plat	[æ]	hat	[t]	ton	[t]	tea
[ɑ]	pâte	[ɑ:]	arm	[k]	cou	[k]	cat
[ɑ̃]	vent	[e]	ten	[b]	bon	[b]	bad
[e]	né	[ɜ]	fur	[d]	don	[d]	did
[ɛ]	lait	[ɪ]	sit	[g]	goût	[g]	got
[ɛ̃]	vin	[i:]	see	[f]	fou	[f]	fall
[i]	lit	[ɔ:]	saw	[s]	sous	[s]	so
[ɔ]	mort	[ɒ]	got	[ʃ]	chou	[ʃ]	she
[o]	beau	[ʊ]	put	[v]	vous	[v]	voice
[ɔ̃]	bon	[u:]	too	[z]	zéro	[z]	zoo
[ø]	peu	[ʌ]	cup	[ʒ]	je	[ʒ]	vision
[œ]	peur			[l]	lent	[l]	lane
[œ̃]	brun			[ʀ]	raie	[r]	red
[u]	cou	DIPHTHONGS		[m]	mon	[m]	man
[y]	vu			[n]	non	[n]	no
		[əʊ]	home	[ɲ]	vigne	[ŋ]	sing
		[aɪ]	five	[ŋ]	dancing	[w]	wet
SEMI-VOWELS		[aʊ]	now			[tʃ]	chin
		[eə]	hair			[j]	yes
[j]	hier, yeux	[ɐɪ]	page			[dʒ]	June
[w]	oui, noix	[ɪə]	near			[θ]	thin
[ɥ]	huile, lui	[ɔɪ]	join			[ð]	then
		[ʊə]	pure			[h]	how

For the convenience of users, this table of IPA phonetic symbols is repeated on p. 77.

In this book, we have chosen to aim for a broad transcription of phonetic sounds as opposed to a narrow transcription which would show all the phonetic details. A broad transcription uses fewer symbols. A narrow transcription can be useful in other contexts but would be unnecessary for the purpose of learning to pronounce a second language. Hence, all transcriptions in this book are broad. Similarly, we have chosen to use and show a 'standard' pronunciation. All languages have varieties, which are often referred to as 'accents' and 'dialects'. Again, the description of these varieties lies outside the scope of this book and we shall deal only with standard French.

Exercises

Exercise 1
Read phonetic English

Read the following text and write it in ordinary orthography.

Example: /ðewind blu: səʊstrɒŋlɪ/ the wind blew so strongly

/ ʃi:wɒzbɪ'gɪnɪŋ təget'verɪtaɪədɒv'sɪtɪŋbaɪhɜ:sistə: ɒnðəbæŋk ændɒvhævɪŋ'nʌθɪŋtʊdu: // wʌnsɔ:rtwaɪs ʃi:hæ dpi:pd 'ɪntuðəbʊk hɜ:sistə:wɒzri:dɪŋ bʌtɪthædnəʊpɪktʃərs ɔ:rkɒnvə'serʃns ɪnɪt // ænd wɒtwɒzðəju:sɒvəbʊk ʃi:'θɔ:t wɪðaʊtpɪktʃərs ɔ:rkɒnvə'serʃns/

Exercise 2
Read phonetic French

Read the following text and write it in ordinary orthography.

Example: / ləvã suflɛfɔʀ dãlavil/ Le vent soufflait fort dans la ville

/ səlakɔmãse alafatige dəʀɛste asizẽsi akote dəsasœʀ syʀlətaly sãzavwaʀ ʀjẽnafɛʀ // ynudøfwa ɛlavɛjəte œ̃kudœjfyʀtif dãləlivʀ kəlizɛ sasœʀ mɛzil nəkɔ̃tnɛ ni ilystʀasjɔ̃ nikɔ̃vɛʀsasjɔ̃ // e akwasɛʀvɛdɔ̃kœ̃livʀ sədizɛtɛl sãzilystʀasjɔ̃ nikɔ̃vɛʀsasjɔ̃/

1. SYLLABLES AND SYLLABIFICATION

A syllable is a unit of pronunciation consisting of a vowel, often with the addition of one or several consonants. In French, the number of syllables in a word is determined by the number of vowels it contains. For example, in the word *court* [kuʀ], since you can hear only the vowel [u], the word has only one syllable: this is a monosyllabic word. In the word *couru* [kuʀy], since you can hear the vowels [u] and [y], the word has two syllables. A single vowel, without adjacent consonants, is a syllable. For example *après* has two syllables, [a] and [pʀɛ]. All syllables have the same values in French and they should all be clearly articulated.

There are two types of syllables: 'open' syllables and 'closed' syllables.

Open syllables

A syllable is called 'open' when it ends with a vocalic sound. For example the word *si* [si] consists of a single open syllable, the word *midi* [mi di] has two open syllables and the word *réparer* [ʀe pa ʀe] has three open syllables. It should be pointed out that in [ʀe pa ʀe] the three phonetic units consist of one consonant followed by a vowel and not the

15

opposite as found commonly in English. This is because
the French language prefers open syllables. Thus a
division such as [ʀep-aʀ-e] would be impossible in
French. Statistical analysis of French speech reveals that
four out of five syllables are open.

Closed syllables

A syllable is called 'closed' when it ends with a consonantal
sound. For example *patte* [pat] consists of a single closed
syllable and *tracteur* [tʀak tœʀ] or *pascal* [pas kal] has
two closed syllables.

　　The emphasis on open syllabification in French
has implications for written French, as the rules of
hyphenation reflect the pattern of the spoken language.
Thus, hyphens are always inserted after the vowel except
in the case of clusters of consonants where they are
placed between the two consonants. For example, the
word *anticonstitutionnel* [ɑ̃ ti kɔ̃s ti ty sjɔ nɛl] will be
hyphenated thus: an-ti-cons-ti-tu-tion-nel.

Exercises

Exercise 1

Organise the words of the following sentences into two lists. Put into list 1 all the words ending in an open syllable and into list 2 all the words ending in a closed syllable. For each word give a transcription in phonetic alphabet.

Example: Il était clair que l'homme ne savait pas courir.

List 1 (open syllables): était /etɛ/, que /kə/, ne /nə/, savait /savɛ/, pas /pa/

List 2 (closed syllables): il /il/, clair /klɛʀ/, l'homme /lɔm/, courir /kuʀiʀ/

Text

Le soir, comme ils rentraient des champs, les parents trouvent le chat sur la margelle du puits où il était occupé à faire sa toilette. « Allons, dirent-ils, voilà le chat qui passe sa patte par-dessus son oreille. Il va encore pleuvoir demain. »

Exercise 2

In the following sentence, split the words into single syllables. Use slashes to indicate the point of division.

Example: Cette remarquable continuité constitutionnelle est toujours perceptible.
Cett(e)/re/mar/quabl(e)/con/ti/nui/té/cons/ti/tu/tio/nnelle/est/tou/jours/per/cep/tibl(e)/

Text

La principale nouveauté sociale du temps est l'apparition du prolétariat industriel, dont les conditions de vie étaient infiniment plus difficiles que celles de l'ouvrier du secteur artisanal.

2. STRESS AND RHYTHM

Stress

Stress is the intensity, or loudness, of the airstream. It can be described as an accentuation or an emphasis put on one syllable, one word or one group of words. This emphasis is most pronounced in vowels. The process of production is complex and involves intensity, pitch and length. The timbre may also be altered. In general, stress is not as strong or as important in French as it is in English.

For the second language learner, French stress is easier to manage than English stress. In English, each word has its own stress which can be fixed either on the first syllable, the last, or any of the syllables in between. In French, you do not have to learn where the word stress is since it is always on the last syllable of the word or group of words.

Compare the following words:

French	English
con for **táble**	**cóm** for ta ble
in té res **sánt**	**ín** te res ting
his to **ríque**	his **tó** ric

In English, morphological or semantic factors determine the position of the stress in the word. A shift of stress can indicate a different grammatical category, as in im **pórt** (verb) and **ím** port (noun). However, once established, the stress remains in the same position in any given word, whatever its position in the sentence.

In French, semantic or grammatical groups of words are considered as units and the stress will be found on the last syllable of the group rather than on the last syllable of each word. For example, the sentence '*Un chien! J'ai vu un chien noir!*' will be stressed thus: 'un **chién**! J'ai vu un chien **nóir**!' [ɛ̃ʃjɛ̃/ jevyɛ̃ʃjɛ̃nwaʀ].

Rhythm

When we speak, we pause from time to time in between groups of words. These are called 'breath groups'. The rhythm arises from the succession of pauses and sequences of syllables. The melody of the French language is determined by the specific patterns of such a rhythm.

Breath groups tend to correspond to semantic and grammatical units.

For example:

> *Elle s'est fait mal.* (1 rhythmic group)
> *Elle s'est fait mal en courant.* (2 rhythmic groups)

Stress is closely related to rhythm since a pause marks the end of a word group which is necessarily stressed on the last syllable. In the above example, *Elle s'est fait mal en courant*, the stress is on the last syllable of each rhythmic group [ɛlsefɛ**mal** ɑ̃kuʀɑ̃].

You will find more details about rhythm in chapter 9 below.

Exercises

Exercise 1
Read the following text and transcribe it in ordinary orthography.

Example: /ɛletɛfjɛʀ dəpɔʀte yn nuvɛlʀɔb/
Elle était fière de porter une nouvelle robe.

Text

/ɑ̃nɛfe ləlɑ̃dmɛ̃ lɑ plɥitɔ̃ba tutlaʒuʀne // ilnəfalɛpa
pɑ̃se a aletʀavaje // faʃedənpuvwaʀ mɛtʀlənedɔɔʀ
lepaʀɑ̃ etɛdmovɛzymœʀ epøpasjɑ̃ avɛklœʀdøfij/

Exercise 2
Transcribe the following groups of words phonetically and indicate the stressed syllable in each group by underlining it.

Example: la belle brune /labɛlbʀyn/

1. Un des spectacles
2. L'aspect général
3. Le peuple français
4. Un vaste champ
5. Une tempête de neige
6. Des visages heureux
7. Je suis fatigué
8. Mais ça va pas !
9. Il fait beau
10. Que me voulez-vous ?

21

3. ORAL VOWELS (1)
Vowels [u], [y], [i], [a], [e], [o] and [ø]

1. The vowel [i]

[i] is the closest front vowel (see the trapezium
of French vowels on p. 9 above). The lips are fully
spread. This is the sound you hear in the word
pipe [pip].

Tips for pronouncing
The [i] in French *six* [sis] is different from the [ɪ] in
English *six* [sɪks]. The lips are more spread when you
pronounce the French word, just as when you smile. In
order to acquire the correct tenseness you can start by
pronouncing the English word *yes* and concentrate on
the first element of the word and making it last longer
until you drop the second element:

yes [jes] ➤ [j - es] ➤ [i - es] ➤ [i].

2. The vowel [u]

[u] is the closest back vowel. The lips are fully rounded.
This is the sound you hear in the word *soupe* [sup].

Tips for pronouncing

When a French speaker says *la soupe* [lasup], the sound [u] is very different from the sound in English *soup* [su:p] which may appear at first to be similar. The difference lies in the fact that a French speaker uses more muscular tenseness than an English speaker. In order to pronounce [u], your lips must be completely rounded. Compare [u] with [i] which, in contrast, requires fully spread lips.

If you look at yourself in a mirror and say *si* [si] and then *sous* [su], your lips are spread in the first instance and then rounded. When you pronounce [i] the tongue is raised towards the hard palate and positioned slightly forward. When you switch to [u], it stays at the same height, but moves slightly backwards and, at the same time, you move your lips to a rounded position. The rounding of the lips even takes place before the articulation of the preceding consonant (this is an instance of the phenomenon of vocalic anticipation mentioned earlier in the introduction). Thus, before articulating the [s] of *sous*, lips and tongue are ready to pronounce the sound [u]. This is a further difference between French *soupe* and English *soup* where such a labialisation does not occur.

3. The vowel [a]

[a] is the most open front vowel. The lips are in a neutral position. This is the sound we hear in *ma* [ma] or *pas* [pa].

Tips for pronouncing

[a] is quite easy to pronounce. It requires little articulation. The mouth is opened, your tongue is lowered and your lips are relaxed in a neutral position.

As a help to producing a correct French [a] (different from English [ɑ:]) you can start by pronouncing the English word *I* [aɪ] (a diphthong consisting of [a] + [ɪ]): concentrate on the first element of the diphthong and drop the second element: *I* [aɪ] ➤ [a-ɪ] ➤ [a].

4. The vowel [e]

[e] is a close-mid front vowel. The lips are spread. This is the sound you hear in the word *café* [kafe].

Tips for pronouncing
Once again this a pure vowel, which maintains its articulation throughout. The lips are spread, though slightly less than for [i], the tongue is positioned towards the front of the mouth. It is important to keep the muscular tenseness to avoid diphthongisation. For the production of 'pure' vowels in *été* [ete], *café* [kafe] or *dé* [de], you should keep your tongue and your lips in the same position while you pronounce [e] so as to avoid gliding towards [i].

5. The vowel [ø]

[ø] is a front close-mid vowel. The lips are rounded. This is the sound you hear in the word *deux* [dø].

Tips for pronouncing
As for [u], rounding of the lips takes place before the articulation of the preceding consonant. To help with the production of a true [ø], you can pronounce [e] as in *dé* [de], and then round your lips. Keep your tongue raised.

6. The vowel [y]

[y] is a front close vowel. The lips are rounded. This is the sound you hear in the words *du* [dy] or *sur* [syʀ].

Tips for pronouncing

English speakers find it difficult to pronounce [y] because there is no corresponding sound in their own language. Furthermore, it requires a significant muscular effort, especially for the position of the lips. It is important to differentiate between the sound [u] as in *sous* and the sound [y] as in *sur*.

Second-language learners from English-speaking countries tend to pronounce French [y] as English [uː], as in the word *super* [suːpə(r)]. But French [y] is nearer to [i]. The lips are fully rounded, as when you whistle. Try to say [i] while keeping your lips rounded or just try to whistle [i]! Alternatively, you may try to pronounce the word *jupe* [ʒyp]. It will be easier to pronounce [y] because your tongue is already in the right position when you articulate the consonant *j* [ʒ].

7. The vowel [o]

[o] is a back close-mid vowel. The lips are rounded. It is the sound you hear in the words *pot* [po] or *beau* [bo].

Tips for pronouncing

As in the other vowels, French [o] requires more muscular effort and tenseness than English sounds [ɔ] and [ʊ]. Compare for example French *oh* [o], as in *oh là là*, with English 'oh' [əʊ] as in 'oh dear!'. Once again, Hiberno-English speakers will find it easier to produce the

French sound [o], since it is part of their range of vowels. For example, in Kerry or Cork, one often hears the [o] in 'hallo' or 'so' sounding like the [o] in French *pot, beau* or *saut*.

For pronouncing [o] the lips must be fully rounded, preferably even before articulating the preceding consonant. The tongue and the jaw must be maintained firmly in the same position so as to avoid diphthongisation as in English *oh* [əʊ] or *mode* [məʊd].

Exercises

Exercise 1
In the following text, which words contain the sound [y] ?

> Six mois plus tard, le vétérinaire de La Voulte reçut du même fermier un appel très inquiet. Une nouvelle vache de son exploitation présentait les mêmes symptômes.
> « Curieux hasard, ai-je simplement pensé. Abcès ?
> Tumeur ? » Au troisième cas, Marcel Soubirou eut une intuition : cela ressemblait au début d'une épidémie.

Exercise 2
In the following text, which words contain the sound [e] ?

> Mais la revue qui a publié la première étude ne dit rien de sa cause ni de son éventuelle transmission.
> On est encore en plein brouillard. Etudes et expériences sont certes diligentées et les ministères concernés tenus au courant mais, curieusement, le problème des conséquences possibles sur l'homme n'est pas à l'ordre du jour. L'infection touche pourtant le poulet, un animal familier, grandement consommé.

Exercise 3

In the following text, which words contain the sound [ø] ?

Je suis heureux. Il n'y a qu'un seul jour où je m'ennuie dans la vie, c'est lorsque je suis obligé d'aller à Paris, une fois par an, parce qu'on a une tante qui invite tous ses neveux et nous sommes tous réunis autour de la table familiale. Mon premier cousin germain n'a jamais connu de bonheur. Il a échoué à tous ses examens, il est devenu masseur, mais il a très peu de clients. Sa femme l'a quitté il y a deux ans. Il n'arrête pas de parler d'argent. Je dois dire qu'il est quelque peu ennuyeux.

Exercise 4

Write the following text phonetically and practise reading it.

La « Série noire » est l'œuvre de ses auteurs, certes, mais aussi de l'équipe de Duhamel qui a su l'imposer par la qualité de ses choix, ses règles de traduction et par l'humour de ses titres. Son succès vient-il de son romantisme noir, de son écriture proche de la peinture cinématographique ou des rêves qu'elle porte ? Elle est aussi l'un des signes d'une France qui se reconstruit et s'initie, à tâtons et sans trop le savoir, au modèle américain.

4. ORAL VOWELS (2)
Vowels [ɛ], [ə], [ɔ], [œ] and [ɑ]

I. The vowel [ɛ]

[ɛ] is a front open-mid vowel. The lips are spread. This is the sound which you hear in the words *mère* [mɛʀ], *pêche* [pɛʃ] or *treize* [tʀɛz].

Tips for pronouncing

This vowel is more open than the vowel [e] described in the previous chapter. In order to pronounce it correctly your lips must be spread but you should also open your mouth wider than when you pronounce [e]. A sound [ɛ] exists in English as in *bread* /brɛd/, but English speakers frequently tend to replace French [ɛ] by the diphthong [eɪ] as in the word *day* [deɪ]. In order to avoid pronouncing the French word *dès* like *day* or *reine* like *rain*, you can practise the following exercise: make the sound [ɛ] with your lips well spread and your mouth clearly opened (as when you pronounce the English word *pan* [pæn]), and keep producing the same sound several times without changing the position of your lower jaw or the position of your tongue.

Distribution of [e] and [ɛ]

[e] and [ɛ] do not have the same distribution. This means that they are usually found in different phonetic environments. As a result, they are rarely in a position of contrast. Here are the main areas of distribution of [e] and [ɛ]:

(a) [ɛ] is found in closed stressed syllables.

père [pɛʀ], *mètre* [mɛtʀ], *fête* [fɛt], *belle* [bɛl], *messe* [mɛs], *assiette* [asjɛt], *faire* [fɛʀ], *laisse* [lɛs].

(b) [e] is found in open stressed syllables.

(i) always in the following cases:

Nouns ending in -*é*, -*ée*, -*er* and -*ez*. For example *été* [ete], *thé* [te], *fumée* [fyme], *vallée* [vale], *marée* [maʀe], *cocher* [kɔʃe], *nez* [ne]

Verbs in the infinitive, past participle and present imperative: *marcher* [maʀʃe], *couché* [kuʃe], *sortez* [sɔʀte]

(ii) more and more in the following two cases, where the traditional pronunciation [ɛ] tends to be replaced by [e] even among the educated population in French cities:

Nouns ending in -*ai*, -*aie*, -*ais*, -*ait*, -*et*.
For example *quai* [kɛ] ➤ [ke] , *taie* [tɛ] ➤ [te], *marais* [maʀɛ] ➤ [maʀe], *lait* [lɛ] ➤ [le], *valet* [valɛ] ➤ [vale]

Verbs in the imperfect indicative and in the present conditional. For example *chantais* [ʃɑ̃tɛ] ➤ [ʃɑ̃te],

30

dansait [dɑ̃sɛ] ➤ [dɑ̃se], *dormirait* [dɔʀmiʀɛ] ➤
[dɔʀmiʀe], *mangerais* [mɑ̃ʒʀɛ] ➤ [mɑ̃ʒʀe].

(c) In unstressed syllables, it is possible to find either
[e] or [ɛ].

Note, however, that in front of a cluster of two
consonants, one uses [ɛ]. For example, *lecture* [lɛktyʀ],
dernier [dɛʀnje], *inepte* [inɛpt], *destin* [dɛstɛ̃]

Because of their distribution, the contrast between
[e] and [ɛ] does not affect the meaning of words and,
depending on regional pronunciation, [e] may be found
for [ɛ] and vice versa.

2. The vowel [ə]

[ə] is a central mid-open vowel. The lips are rounded.
This is the sound you hear in the words *mener* [məne],
rechercher [ʀəʃɛʀʃe], *semer* [səme] or *cela* [səla].

Tips for pronouncing
This vowel is quite easy to pronounce for English
speakers since French [ə] is similar to English [ə] which
you hear in *gala* [gɑ:lə] or *ever* [evə(r)]. However, the
French sound requires some effort of articulation and
your lips must be rounded.

3. The vowel [ɔ]

[ɔ] is a back mid-open vowel. The lips are rounded. This
is the sound you hear in *note* [nɔt], *botte* [bɔt], *hotte* [hɔt]
or *bol* [bɔl].

31

Tips for pronouncing

When pronouncing words like *note* or *botte*, English speakers tend to produce the sound [ɒ] which you hear in *not* [nɒt] or *hot* [hɒt]. [ɒ] is a back vowel which is more open than [ɔ]. You can correct this by rounding your lips and moving your tongue up towards the centre as if you were going to pronounce [ə]. For example, if you try to pronounce the word *joli*, the correct pronunciation will be somewhere between [ʒɒli] and [ʒəli], although slightly nearer to the latter.

Distribution of [ɔ] and [o]

Like [e] and [ɛ], [o] and [ɔ] are found in different environments.

(*a*) [o] is always found in open stressed syllables.

For example, *mot* [mo], *sot* [so], *dos* [do], *beau* [bo], *faux* [fo], *accroc* [akʀo].

(*b*) In closed stressed syllables

    (i) [o] is found

    before the sound [z]. For example, *rose* [ʀoz], *chose* [ʃoz], *cause* [koz].

    in words spelled with -*au*-, -*eau*- and -*ô*-. For example, *saute* [sot], *faute* [fot], *heaume* ['om], *hôte* ['ot], *rôle* [ʀol], *côte* [kot].

    (ii) [ɔ] is found in all the other cases

    For example, *col* [kɔl], *sotte* [sɔt], *cote* [kɔt], *homme* [ɔm], *hotte* ['ɔt], *fort* [fɔʀ] (*c*) In unstressed syllables [ɔ] is generally found.

For example *moderne* [mɔdɛʀn], *promettre* [pʀɔmɛtʀ], *hippopotame* [ipɔpɔtɑm], *logis* [lɔʒi].

Again, as in the case of [e] and [ɛ], because the contrast between [o] and [ɔ] is not significant for the meaning of words, [o] will be used for [ɔ] and vice versa depending on regional or social origin.

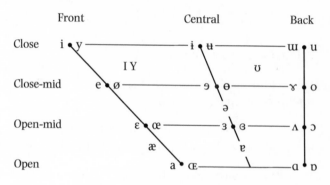

IPA symbols: vowels

4. The vowel [œ]

[œ] is open-mid front vowel. The lips are rounded. This is the sound you hear in *peur* [pœʀ], *beurre* [bœʀ], *oeuf* [œf], *neuf* [nœf].

Tips for pronouncing
Instead of [œ] English speakers tend to produce the sound [ɜ:] which is found in *fur* [fɜ:(r)] or in *word* [wɜ:d]. [ɜ] is a central vowel, more akin to [ə] than to [œ], which is positioned more to the front. In order to compensate for this tendency, try the following exercise: pronounce [ɛ] ,

33

and then round your lips as if pronouncing [ɔ]. You should end up with a sound approaching [œ]. Try contrasting *pair* [pɛʀ] and *peur* [pœʀ], *mère* [mɛʀ] and *meurt* [mœʀ], *nef* [nɛf] and *neuf* [nœf].

Contrast between [œ] et [ø] and between [ø] et [ə]
The distribution of [œ] et [ø] is as follows:

(*a*) [ø] is always found in open stressed syllables

For example *feu* [fø], *peu* [pø], *deux* [dø], *ceux* [sø]

(*b*) In closed stressed syllables

(i) [ø] is found before the sound [z] *peureuse* [pœʀøz], *heureuse* [œʀøz], *liseuse* [lizøz]

(ii) [œ] is found before [ʀ] and the semi-vowel [j] *heure* [œʀ], *soeur* [sœʀ], *feuille* [fœj], *deuil* [dœj]

(iii) in other environments, both [œ] and [ø] can occur.

It is easy to confuse the sounds [ø] and [ə] which are quite similar both in acoustic and articulatory terms. The difference which is best perceived between these two sounds is one of length. The vowel [ø] is clearly longer than [ə]. It is mostly length which allows us to distinguish between *ceux* [sø] and *ce* [sə], *jeu* [ʒø] and *je* [ʒə], *noeud* [nø] and *ne* [nə], *queue* [kø] and *que* [kə].

5. The vowel [ɑ]

[ɑ] is an open back vowel. This sound is becoming rarer and rarer in French, especially among the educated urban population who tended to use it most. However,

French people try to preserve it in order to avoid confusion of meaning in words like *tâche* [tɑʃ] (≠ *tache* [taʃ]) or *mâle* [mɑl] (≠*malle* [mal]).

Tips for pronouncing

In order to pronounce [ɑ], you need to lower your tongue as much as possible and clearly open your lips without spreading them. Actually, the French sound [ɑ] is quite close to English [ɑ] which you hear in the words *bar* [bɑ:(r)] or *calm* [kɑ:m].

Contrast between [ɑ] and [a]

Contrast between these two sounds may be found in all positions. The following table gives a list of instances where contrast between the two sounds is necessary in order to avoid confusion between words with different meaning.

[a]	[ɑ]
chasse	châsse
la / là	las
malle	mâle
patte	pâte
poil	poêle
tache	tâche

Exercises

Exercise 1
In the following text, which words contain the sound [ə]?

J'étais revenu au pays de mes ancêtres. Quand j'avais traversé le village, tout le monde s'était mis aux fenêtres comme si c'était la première fois qu'ils voyaient un étranger. Je ne me croyais pas un homme si curieux. Cela me fit résoudre de repartir le plus vite possible en regrettant de ne pouvoir rester deux jours de plus pour visiter le château de mon aieul.

Exercise 2
In the following text, which words contain the sound [œ]?

« A la bonne heure ! » m'écriais-je en voyant le visage heureux de ma soeur dans l'embrasure de la porte. Le vieux chien aveugle avait reconnu son pas et lui faisait fête. Elle était suivie d'un jeune homme qui tenait une lettre à la main. « C'est le facteur ! » cria-t-il joyeusement. Je les fis entrer tous les deux et leur proposai du café au lait et une tartine de beurre.

Exercise 3
Give two spellings for each pronunciation.

Example: /so/: sot, seau, sceau.

List

1. /po/	6. /prɛ/
2. /mo/	7. /to/
3. /a/	8. /sɔ̃/
4. /sə/	9. /o/
5. /ɔ̃/	10. /dɑ̃/

ORAL VOWELS (2)

Exercise 4

Read the following text and write in ordinary orthography.

/məsjølənwaʀ ɑ̃tʀadɑ̃lapjɛs sɑ̃səʀətuʀne puʀvwaʀ
sisafamləsɥivɛ // setɛ̃ɛ̃natəlje dəʀepaʀ̃sjɔ̃ ? *et sol était*
dəmotœʀelɛktʀik eləsɔletɛkuvɛʀ debudəfil *couvert de*
dətutkulœʀ // laʒœnfam fytetɔne paʀlavy dezɑ̃tʀaj *bout de*
dapaʀɛjmenaʒe kɛlkɔnɛsɛbjɛ̃ edɔ̃tɛlnəsupsɔnɛpa *fils de*
lakɔ̃plɛksite demekanismɛ̃tɛʀjœʀ // ləʃɛfdekip *toutes les*
sələva dəsɔ̃netabli esavɑ̃sa vɛʀməsjølenwaʀ puʀlɥi
seʀelamɛ̃ /.

Exercise 5

Write the following text phonetically.

Nous n'étions pas sûr de rejoindre la côte. J'avais envoyé
un message radio au port pour qu'on nous envoie un
bateau de sauvetage. Les vagues étaient de plus en plus
hautes et la chaloupe prenait l'eau. Nous commencions
à avoir peur. «Encore heureux qu'il fasse encore jour»,
cria Paul pour briser un silence qui devenait lourd.
A peine eut-il parlé qu'apparut à bâbord la vedette
des garde-côtes de l'Île Noire.

5. NASAL VOWELS

As we have seen, some vowels in French are called nasal vowels. Behind the hard palate (in the roof of your mouth) is the soft palate or velum. If the soft palate is raised the nasal cavity is closed off and the sound is oral (or non nasal). If the soft palate is lowered, the air escapes through the nasal cavity (as well as the mouth) and the resulting sound is nasal. The nasal vowels in French are [ɑ̃], [ɛ̃], [ɔ̃] and [œ̃]. In the phonetic alphabet (IPA), nasality is indicated by the diacritic sign [˜]. You will notice that today the nasal sound [œ̃] is tending to disappear from French and is replaced by [ɛ̃]. People variably say /œ̃juʀ/ (*un jour*) and /ɛ̃juʀ/.

Tips for pronouncing
These four vowels are made in almost exactly the same way. The main feature which distinguishes one from the other is the position of the lips and tongue.

To pronounce [ɛ̃] the lips are not rounded; for [ɑ̃] they are not rounded but they are very open and for [ɔ̃] the lips are rounded as for [ɔ], but more open.

If you try and say *le bon vin blanc* without moving your lips, you will find that it is impossible to do. That is because it is precisely the movement of the lips which is essential for the articulation of these sounds.

39

Nasality exists in all languages, but in French nasality is not 'diffuse'. In English, for example, vowels are affected by neighbouring consonants. In the English word *pan* /pæn/ the nasal consonant /n/diffuses onto the preceding vowel and the /a/ is nasalised. In the French word *panne* /pan/ the nasal consonant does not influence the preceding vowel and /a/ remains an oral sound.

Learners whose first language is English need to be careful that nasality remains only on the nasal sounds and does not diffuse onto other sounds. The vowels in *panne, bonne* and *lune* are the same as those in *patte, botte* and *luge*. So that your nasal sound does not affect others, you can make a little pause between the vowel and the nasal sound which follows it. For example: pa-nne, bo-nne, lu-ne.

It is important to remember that nasal vowels matter in French, because they make a difference in meaning:

/bo/ does not mean the same thing as /bɔ̃/ (*beau ≠ bon*)
/pa/ does not mean the same as /pɑ̃/ (*pas ≠ pend*)
/tɑ/ does not mean the same as /tɑ̃/ (*ta ≠ temps*).

Nasality can make the difference between masculine and feminine in French. [ɛ̃] is not [ɛn]. Anglophones tend to confuse these two. In French, as we have seen, the sound /n/ must not affect the preceding [ɛ]. *Marie est Americaine*, /-kɛn/, mais *Paul est Americain* /kɛ̃/.

Exercises

Exercise 1
Which nasal sounds do the following proper names contain?
Léon, Alain, Gaston, Constance, Sébastien, Simon, Julien, Henri.

Exercise 2
Pronounce the following pairs of words. Notice that in the French words the final consonant does not affect the preceding vowel:

English	French
Jan	Jeanne
pan	panne
can	canne
fan	fane
van	vanne

Exercise 3
Here is a series of words. Make a gap between the oral vowel and the following sound. (You can test that you are doing this properly by pinching your nose and making sure you feel no vibration while making the vowel sound.)

- bo-nne
- mi-ne
- lu-ne
- tie-nne
- sai-ne
- co-mme
- so-mme
- assu-me
- l'â-me

Exercise 4.
As we said earlier, nasality can affect meaning. [ɛ̃] is not the same as [ɛn]. [ɛ̃] is a nasal vowel; [ɛn] is two sounds: an oral vowel followed by [n]. In French, the difference in sound

41

between [ɛ̃] and [ɛn] can make a difference between masculine and feminine.

Repeat the following phrases:

Anne est Canadienne. Son mari est Canadien.
Claire est Américaine. Son mari est Américain.
Malika est Marocaine. Son mari est Marocain.
Nadia est Algérienne. Son mari est Algérien.
Amina est Égyptienne. Son mari est Égyptien.
Claudine est Parisienne. Son mari est Parisien.
Fatima est Tunisienne. Son mari est Tunisien.
Maria est Mexicaine. Son mari est Mexicain.

6. GLIDE APPROXIMANTS

L sounds, *r* sounds and 'glides' are called approximants because they do not have full oral closure as in oral and nasal stops and fricatives.

Semi-vowels (glides), also called semi-consonants, have some of the characteristics of both vowels and consonants. They have a vocalic quality and they are very closed but, on the other hand, they are so closed that they produce a friction like the constrictive consonants. There are three semi-vowels in French: /j/, /w/ and /ɥ/.

1. The sound /j/

This is the palatal sound which occurs in *payer* /peje/, *piano* /pjano/ or *paille* /paj/.

Tips for pronouncing
In initial position, English speakers have no difficulty as /j/ is the same sound as the one in words like *yard* /jɑ:d/, *yell* /jel/ or *you* /ju:/.

In final position, it is very close to the English diphthong /aɪ/ as in *why* /waɪ/ or *wild* /waɪld/, so if you say *pie* in English you are close to French *paille* /paj/.

After a consonant, it is easy to confuse the sound /j/ alone, with the combination /i/ + /j/. For example, the

word *lier* is pronounced /lje/ in one single syllable
whereas *plier* is pronounced /plije/ in two syllables.
There is no absolute rule as regards the distribution of
these two sound units. However, in general we can say:

➤ /j/ is pronounced

(*a*) when the semi-vowel is between two vowels:
payer /peje/, *tailleur* /tajœʀ/, *joyeux* /jwajø/.

(*b*) when the semi-vowel follows one single initial
consonant within a single syllable: *avion* (a-vion) /avjɔ̃/
panier (pa-nier) /panje/, *papier* (pa-pier) /papje/,
premier (pre-mier) /pʀemje/.

➤ /ij/ is pronounced

when the semi-vowel is preceded by at least
two consonants in its own syllable: *plier* /plije/,
trier /tʀije/, *client* /klijɑ̃/, *oublier* (ou-blier) /ublije/,
bibliothèque (bi-bliothèque) /biblijotɛk/.

2. The sound /w/

This is the sound found in words like *oui* /wi/, *ouest* /wɛst/,
oiseau /wazo/, *boire* /bwaʀ/, *voiture* /watyʀ/, *louer* /lwe/,
bouée /bwe/.

Tips for pronouncing
In initial position there is generally no problem for
anglophones, as /w/ is very like the familiar sound we
hear in *wind* /wɪnd/, *west* /west/ or *work* /wɜ:k/.
However, it is important to notice that the French
semi-vowel is labial and that the lips are much more
rounded than when we say English /w/.

The spelling -oi- represents the sound /wa/ as in *bois* /bwa/, *roi* /ʀwa/, *choix* /ʃwa/, *noix* /nwa/, *trois* /tʀwa/, *croix* /kʀwa/.

Note that syllables in words like these are divided up in the following way:

louer /lwe/ (one syllable) and *clouer* /klu- e / (two syllables)

rouer /ʀwe/ (one syllable) and *trouer* /tʀu- e / (two syllables)

enfouir /ã-fwiʀ/ (2 syllables) and *renflouer* (ren-flouer) /ʀã-flu- e / (3 syllables).

You will notice that in syllables where the initial consonant is single, it is usually followed by the semi-vowel /w/, whereas initial consonants which are multiple are usually followed by the vowel /u/. When in doubt consult your dictionary.

3. The sound /ɥ/

This is the palatal sound which is found in words like *lui* /lɥi/, *huit* /ɥit/, *suivre* /sɥivʀ/, *s'enfuir* /sãfɥiʀ/, *pluie* /plɥi/, *bruit* /bʀɥi/, *sueur* /sɥœʀ/, *tuer* /tɥe/.

Tips for pronouncing
This semi-vowel is labial so to pronounce it you need to round your lips as if you were getting ready to say /y/. Your tongue is placed very high in the mouth, almost against the hard palate. The articulation of /ɥ/ is difficult for English speakers and so it is important to have already learnt to make the sound /y/. A frequent mistake of English speakers is to place the tongue at the back in position for /u/ rather than placing it in front in position

45

for /y/. The distinction for these two sounds allows one to avoid confusions of meaning in words such as:

bouée /bwe/ and *buée* /bɥe/
dénoué /denwe/ and *dénué* /denɥe/
loueur /lwœʀ/ and *lueur* /lɥœʀ/
Louis /lwi/ and *lui* /lɥi/
nouée /nwe/ and *nuée* /nɥe/
rouet /ʀwe/ and *ruée* /ʀɥe/
souhait /swɛ/ and *suait* /sɥɛ/

Exercises

Exercise 1
Indicate which glides are contained in the following words:
Oui, puis, tuer, louer, feuille, fruit, mouette, lier, famille, ouate, oiseau, Louise, payer, hier.

Exercise 2
Make a broad phonetic transcription of the following passage.

Cette nuit, la ville est calme, il fait noir et le vent vient de l'ouest. Louis somnole sous sa couette. Dans les ruelles, une jeune fille poursuit son chemin sous la lune brillante. Il est huit heures. Soudain, le portail s'ouvre. Louis tend l'oreille. Il essaie d'entendre la fille entrer dans la cour.

7. THE CONSONANTS /p/, /t/, /k/ AND /b/, /d/, /g/

Vowels are made with no interruption in the flow of air which comes from the lungs and escapes through the nose and mouth. When we pronounce a consonant, on the other hand, there is an interruption in this passage of air.

1. Stops and fricatives

The interruption in the airstream does not happen in the same way for all consonants. Pronounce the two sounds /s/ and /t/ one after the other ➤ /st/. While you are saying /s/, there is an interruption in the passage of air. Nevertheless, the air continues to flow until the sound /t/ is pronounced, at which moment there is a complete interruption. In the case of /p/, /t/, /k/, /b/, /d/, /g/, there is a complete blockage of the airstream by the mouth. These sounds are called 'stops'. Where the interruption is only partial, in the case of /f/, /v/, /s/, /z/, /ʃ/ and /ʒ/, the result is a 'fricative'.

2. Voiced and voiceless consonants

Consonants are either voiced or voiceless. Try saying /s/ and afterwards /z/ keeping your hand lightly on your throat. You will notice that for /s/ your vocal cords (or vocal folds) do not vibrate and for /z/ they do vibrate. /s/ is a voiceless sound while /z/ is voiced. In fact, we can say that /z/ is the same as /s/ plus voice. The voiceless consonants are: p, t, k, f, s, while the voiced consonants are: b, d, g, v, z.

3. The articulation of consonants

The articulation of stops consists of three stages:

1. Implosion, when the organs of articulation are put in place.
2. Holding, where this pressure is contained.
3. Explosion, when this air is released.

In fricatives, the final stage is only partial.

The consonants /p/, /t/, /k/

The main difference between these consonants in French and in English is that in English, when they are in initial position in the word, they are followed by a tiny breath which is called an 'aspiration', as in pin /p'ɪn/. This aspiration does not exist in French.

Tips for pronouncing

Hold your hand in front of your mouth while you say: *pin, pen, Peter*. You will feel a little puff of air after each /p/. Now say in French: *pas, pot, Pierre*. You should not feel this puff of air.

48

In French, the vowel has an effect on the preceding consonant (this is called vocalic anticipation). For instance when saying (French) *pot*, at the same moment one is saying /p/, one is already putting the lips in position for saying /o/. This is precisely what avoids the aspiration between the consonant and the vowel. In English, the aspiration always appears in initial position of the word. In fact, the /p/ in the middle of an English word is like the French /p/ (for example *spot* /spɒt/. English learners of French should therefore try to use this /p/ throughout.

The consonants /t/ and /d/
/t/ and /d/ in English are alveolar: that is the tip of the tongue is in contact with the alveolar ridge which is behind the teeth. In French, on the contrary, consonants are dental (the tip of the tongue touches the teeth) The sound is made (and this is true in general for all sounds in French) further forward in the mouth.

Tips for pronouncing
Try and say *tique* /tik/ in French and *tick* /tɪk/ in English. You will find that the tongue moves back to make the English sound.

Exercises

Exercise 1
Make a transcription of the following sentences:

1. C'est quand qu'il arrive ?
2. C'est comment qu'elle fait ça ?
3. Qui est-ce qui l'a vu ?
4. C'est combien, ce livre ?

Exercise 2
Make a transcription of the following sentences:

1. C'est Papa qui a fait cette poule au pot.
2. Paul a pris mon porte-monnaie.
3. Patricia a porté ce panier.
4. C'est Pierre qui a payé le pot.

Exercise 3
Make a transcription of the following sentences:

1. Tu veux du thé ?
2. Tu veux une tartine ?
3. Tu veux des toasts ?
4. Tu veux une tranche de Tomme ?

Exercise 4
Make a transcription of the following sentences:

1. Brigitte l'a balayé avec une branche.
2. La belle Barbara est brune.
3. Blanche se brosse les dents.
4. Bernard est brave et bon.

8. THE CONSONANTS /ʀ/ AND /l/

The consonant 'r'

The sound /ʀ/ that we hear most frequently in French is a uvular sound. The uvula (the very end of the soft palate) vibrates against the back of the tongue. This is called a uvular roll 'r'. If the space is so narrow that the uvula does not vibrate, there is a constriction: this is called a uvular fricative 'r'.

In standard English, on the other hand, 'r' is pronounced by placing the front part of the tongue against the alveolar ridge (behind the front teeth). The place of articulation is obviously very different from the French one.

The distribution of the sound 'r' is also different. In English the 'r' in final position is almost not pronounced. In French, on the other hand, the final 'r' of *car* /kaʀ/ is a uvular fricative 'r'.

Tips for pronouncing
To pronounce a French 'r', first say 'aga, aga'. The tongue keeps the same back position. Then practise pronouncing words in which 'r' is between /a/ and /o/, as in *carafe* /kaʀaf/, *arabe* /aʀab/, *oraux* /oʀo/,

51

parapet /paʀape/. It is almost like the sound you make when you gargle!

The consonant 'l'

In general we can say that in English there are two types of 'l' and in French there is only one. This is a slight over simplification, but is a useful distinction for the learner. In English we say there is a 'clear l' and a 'dark l'. In French there is only a 'clear l'. To articulate this sound, the tip of the tongue is firmly held against the alveolar ridge, and the air escapes by the sides of the tongue. This is why we say that 'l' is a lateral consonant.

The 'clear l' in French which we hear in the proper name *Line* /lin/ is very close to /l/ of *lean* in English. In English, however, there is another /l/ which appears in final position in words like *dull* /dʌl/ or *pull* /pʊl/ and in front of a consonant as in *field* /fi:ld/ or *lilt* /lɪlt/. The Anglophone learner should try therefore to pronounce a 'clear' /l/ throughout in French.

Tips for pronouncing
You can practise saying /l/ followed by the vowels /i/ or /a/ as in *il y vient* /ilivjɛ̃/ or *il a fait* /ilafɛ/. The pronounciation of /l/ in final position will be easier if you follow it by the vowel /i/. For example for *poule*, /pul/, try first saying /pu-li/, with the /l/ as the initial sound of the second syllable. Then little by little, say /ə/ instead of /i/ and eventually pronounce only /pul/. When you articulate /i/ you can manage to keep the tongue in the correct position.

Exercises

Exercise 1
Read the following pairs of words – the first in English, the second in French. Notice the difference in the [l] sounds.

English	French
Ill	il
peel	pile
seal	cil
pal	pale
cool	coule
fool	foule
Sal	salle
film	film
filter	filtre
sultan	sultan

Exercise 2
Practise your /ʀ/ sounds.

Talk about tomorrow.

For example:

> Il prépare son cours.
> Demain, il préparera son cours.

Now try:

1. Elle gare sa voiture.
2. Il arrive ce soir.
3. Marie peut partir.
4. Je ris maintenant.
5. Hélène rentre aujourd'hui.
6. Pierre revient bientôt.
7. Je vois ce film cet après-midi.
8. Elle finit de travailler.

9. LIAISONS

Liaison is the process whereby we pronounce the final consonant of a word, which is normally silent, when it is followed by a word beginning with a vowel. For example, *trop* /tʀo/ has a silent final consonant, but in *trop aimable* /tʀope mabl/ the sound 'p' is pronounced.

When combined with a vowel, some consonants undergo modifications.

1. Voicing

-s /s/ and x /ks/ become /z/

ils aiment /ilzɛm /, *les autres* /lezo tʀ/, *de beaux enfants* /dəbozɑ̃fɑ̃/, *dix amis* /dizami/

-f /f/ can become /v/

neuf ans /nœvɑ̃/, *neuf heures* /nœvœʀ/ (but *neuf enfants* /nœfɑ̃fɑ̃/)

2. Devoicing

-d /d/ becomes /t/

le grand arbre /ləgʀɑ̃taʀbʀ/, *quand il chante* /kɑ̃tilʃɑ̃t/

55

-g /g/ becomes /k/, but this liaison is now very rare.

j'ai sué sang et eau /ʒesɥesɑ̃keo/

3. Denasalisation

/ɛ̃/ can become /ɛn/ and /ɔ̃/ can become /ɔn/.

In the case of a masculine adjective like *bon* /bɔ̃/ followed by a word which starts with a vowel, the pronounciation is the same as for its feminine equivalent. For example the word *bon* in *un bon enfant* /ɛ̃bɔnɑ̃fɑ̃/ is pronounced in the same way as in *une bonne enfant* /ynbɔnɑ̃fɑ̃/. Compare the following examples:

> *un bon ami* /ɛ̃bɔnami/ and *une bonne amie* /ynbɔnami/
> *le moyen âge* /ləmwajɛnaʒ/ and *la moyenne époque* /lamwajɛnepok/
> *en plein air* /ɑ̃plɛnɛʀ/ and *en pleine erreur* /ɑ̃plɛnɛʀœʀ/
> *un certain âge* /ɛ̃sɛʀtɛnaʒ/ and *une certaine attitude* /ynsɛʀtɛnatityd/
> *le prochain arrêt* /ləpʀɔʃɛnaʀɛ/ and *la prochaine étape* /lapʀɔʃɛnetap/

Note, however, that the nasal sound is maintained in liaisons after the words *un, aucun, commun, rien, bien, combien, en, on, mon, ton, son*. For example:

> *un ami* /ɛ̃nami/, *aucun accident* /okɛ̃naksidɑ̃/, *d'un commun accord* /dɛ̃kɔmɛ̃nakoʀ/ *rien à faire* /ʀjɛ̃nafɛʀ/, *bien entendu* /bjɛ̃nɑ̃tɑ̃dy/ *en avant* /ɑ̃navɑ̃/, *on arrive* /ɔ̃naʀiv/, *mon ami* /mɔ̃nami/

Liaison is a complex phenomenon. As well as the phonetic dimension, it is affected by historical and social factors, syntactic relations between words and nuances of meaning. In practice, there are three sorts of liaison: obligatory liaison, proscribed liaison and optional liaison.

Liaison is obligatory

1. between a qualifier (article, pronoun, adjective) and the thing qualified (adjective or noun)

un ami /ɛ̃nami/, *les amis* /lezami/ *nos amis* /nozami/ *nos autres amis* /nozotʀzami/, *deux anciens amis* /døzɑ̃sjɛ̃zami/

2. between a verb and the personal pronouns of the same syntactic unit

nous avons /nuzavɔ̃/, *ils aiment* /ilzɛm /, *aiment-elles* /ɛmtɛl/, *allons-y* /alɔ̃zi /, *nous y allons* /nuzjalɔ̃/, *allons nous-en* /alɔ̃nuzɑ̃/ *on ira* /ɔ̃niʀa /, *dira-t-on* /diʀatɔ̃/.

3. between adverbs or monosyllabic prepositions and the words which follow them

chez elles /ʃezɛl/, *dans un an* /dɑ̃z ɛ̃ ɑ̃/, *sans enfants* /sɑ̃zɑ̃fɑ̃/, *sous un chêne*/suzɛ̃ʃɛn/ *plus adroit* /plyzadʀwa/, *tout essoufflé* /tutɛsufle/, *très aimable* /tʀɛzɛmabl/

4. after *quand* and *dont*

Quand on voit ça . . . /kɑ̃tɔ̃vwasa/, *celle dont il parle* /sɛldɔ̃tilpaʀl/

57

5. in the majority of ready made expressions and words of two or more elements. For example:

> *Avant-hier* /avɑ̃ t j ɛʀ/, *le cas échéant* /ləkazeʃeɑ̃/
> *les Champs-Elysées* /leʃɑ̃zelize/, *comment allez-vous*
> /kɔmɑ̃talevu/, *d'un bout à l'autre* /dɛ̃butalotʀ/,
> *de haut en bas* /dəotɑ̃ba/, *de mieux en mieux*
> /dmjøzɑ̃mjø/, *de plus en plus* /dəplyzɑ̃ply/,
> *de temps en temps* /dətɑ̃zɑ̃tɑ̃/, *du tout au tout*
> /dytutotu/, *les États-Unis* /lezetazy ni/,
> *mot-à-mot* /motamo/, *sous entendu* /suzɑ̃tɑ̃dy/,
> *tout-à-coup* /tutaku/, *vis-à-vis* /vizavi/

Liaisons do not occur

1. in front of words beginning with *h* 'aspiré'. These are usually words of Germanic origin like *la hache* /la aʃ/, *la haine* /la ɛn/, *une halte* /yn alt/, *un havre* /ɛ̃ avʀ/, *le houblon* /lə ublɔ̃/, *une hutte* /yn yt/. On the other hand, in front of words of Latin origin beginning with *h*, liaison is possible as in *un hopital* /ɛ̃nopital/, *un homme* /ɛ̃nɔm /, *une huile* /ynɥil/, *un hôtel* /ɛ̃notɛl/. You can find a complete list of French words beginning with a *h* 'aspiré' in M. Grevisse, *Le bon usage* (Paris, Duculot, 1991) § 101.

2. in front of numeral adjectives *un, huit* and *onze*

> *sur les une heure* /syʀle ynœʀ/, *après huit heures* /apʀɛ ɥitœʀ/, *les onze hommes* /le ɔ̃zɔm/

3. in front of *oui*

> *mais oui* /me wi/, *c'est oui ou non* /se wi u nɔ̃/

4. after *et*

    un chat et un âne /ɛ̃ʃa e ɛ̃nan/, to be compared with
    c'est un âne /setɛ̃nan/

5. after a noun in the singular

    un loup affamé /ɛ̃lu afame/, *un discours intéressant*
    /ɛ̃diskuʀɛ̃teʀɛsɑ̃/, *le coup est parti* /ləku epaʀti/

6. after proper names

    Charles ira en France /ʃaʀl iʀa ɑ̃fʀɑ̃s/, *Paris est*
    grand /paʀi egʀɑ̃/

7. after the internal 's' in the plural of compound words

    les arcs-en-ciel /lezaʀkɑ̃sjɛl/, *les salles à manger*
    /lesalamɑ̃ʒe/.

Optional liaisons

Liaisons are optional in general between words which
are unified by meaning (subject and verb, verb and
object, auxiliary verb and past participle). For example,
les gens arrivent /leʒɑ̃zaʀiv/ or /leʒɑ̃ aʀiv/; *je crois*
entendre /ʒəkʀwazɑ̃tɑ̃dʀ/ or /ʒəkʀwa ɑ̃tɑ̃dʀ/, *je suis*
épuisé /ʒəsɥizepɥize/ or /ʒəsɥi epɥize/. In the case of
optional liaison, the choice to use it or not depends on
the linguistic register one is using. In spontaneous
everyday speech there are few liaisons. However, in
official speech, in a lecture or public speaking, liaison
will be more frequent. It is generally true to say that the
more formal the register, the more the speaker tends to
use liaison.

Exercises

Exercise 1
Make a transcription of the following passage.

> Cette nuit, tout le village est sous la lune. Il gèle. Il est huit
> heures. Au premier étage, les bons amis se disent au revoir.
> « C'est ton anniversaire demain, Paul. On fait une fête,
> chez Pierre et Renée? C'est sympathique chez eux – mais
> sans les autres amis, bien entendu ! N'oubliez pas Marie,
> elle a ses petites habitudes ». « Les gens arriveront tard,
> je crois. Ils seront épuisés après leur travail ».

Exercise 2
In the same passage indicate (*a*) any optional liaisons
(*b*) obligatory liaisons.

10. RHYTHM AND INTONATION

In the course of ordinary conversation, every complex utterance is divided by pauses between groups of words. The succession of pauses and sounds form speech rhythms. Written language tries to imitate these pauses by punctuation. The pause can be single (/) or double (//) according to the meaning the speaker wishes to give his speech. The following sentence illustrates these two types of pause: *Hier, à cinq heures, c'est moi qui me suis levé. Demain, ce sera toi.* [jɛʀ / asɛ̃kœʀ / sɛmwakimsɥilve // dɛmɛ̃ / səsʀatwa]. Rhythmic groups separated by pauses generally correspond to semantic or grammatical units.

As well as the rhythm, intonation also forms part of the utterance. This consists of modulations in tone created by variation in the frequency of vocalic sounds. It is the quality of this frequency which is called 'pitch'. Pitch can vary according to individual or social or regional group, but generally speaking certain intonation curves correspond to certain types of utterance. For instance, the following intonative curve corresponds to the everyday declarative sentence:

Monsieur Dupont ouvrait ses volets.

An interrogative type sentence will have a different intonative pattern.

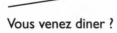

Vous venez diner ?

There are three principal types of intonative curves: rising-falling, rising, and falling.

Rising-falling

This is the pattern found in declarative sentences in speech:

Le bon père de famille prend soin de ses enfants.

Tips for pronouncing
This pattern corresponds to the logical grammatical structure of the sentence and the highest point of the curve varies according to the nature of the sentence uttered.

In simple sentences
1. When the subject is a pronoun

(*a*) if there is no object or if the object is a pronoun, the intonation rises until the second last syllable and falls on the last:

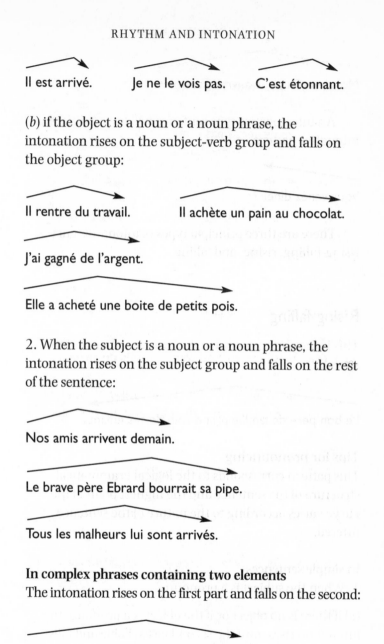

Il est arrivé.   Je ne le vois pas.   C'est étonnant.

(*b*) if the object is a noun or a noun phrase, the intonation rises on the subject-verb group and falls on the object group:

Il rentre du travail.   Il achète un pain au chocolat.

J'ai gagné de l'argent.

Elle a acheté une boite de petits pois.

2. When the subject is a noun or a noun phrase, the intonation rises on the subject group and falls on the rest of the sentence:

Nos amis arrivent demain.

Le brave père Ebrard bourrait sa pipe.

Tous les malheurs lui sont arrivés.

In complex phrases containing two elements
The intonation rises on the first part and falls on the second:

Tant qu'il y a de la vie, il y a de l'espoir.

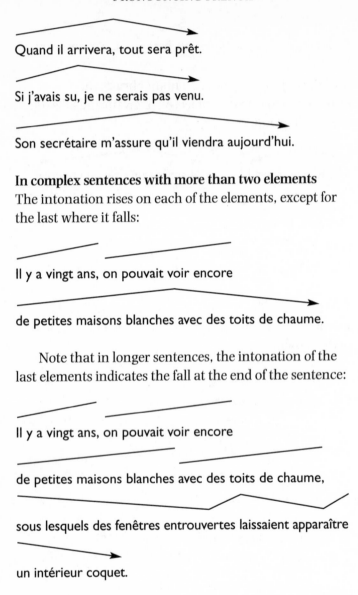

Quand il arrivera, tout sera prêt.

Si j'avais su, je ne serais pas venu.

Son secrétaire m'assure qu'il viendra aujourd'hui.

In complex sentences with more than two elements
The intonation rises on each of the elements, except for
the last where it falls:

Il y a vingt ans, on pouvait voir encore

de petites maisons blanches avec des toits de chaume.

Note that in longer sentences, the intonation of the
last elements indicates the fall at the end of the sentence:

Il y a vingt ans, on pouvait voir encore

de petites maisons blanches avec des toits de chaume,

sous lesquels des fenêtres entrouvertes laissaient apparaître

un intérieur coquet.

The falling pattern

This is the pattern found:

(*a*) in interrogative sentences which begin with an interrogative pronoun

Quand allez-vous sortir ?   Qui allez-vous voir ?

Tips for pronouncing
The highest sound is the interrogative pronoun.
After this the intonative pattern falls until the last syllable.

(*b*) in imperative sentences

Sortez de là !   Donnez-moi vos papiers !

The rising pattern

This pattern is found:

(*a*) in interrogative sentences in the affirmative (the word order is subject + verb)

Vous venez souvent ici ?   Vous aimez ça ?

(*b*) in interrogative sentences with inversion of the subject (the word order is verb + subject)

Aimez-vous la musique classique ?

Connaissez-vous la Navarre ?

Tips for pronouncing
To ask this type of question, you need to start the
sentence at a medium pitch and gradually heighten the
pitch until you reach the last syllable.

Exercises

Exercise 1
Make a broad phonetic transcription of the following text.
Then indicate a possible intonative pattern.

> Paul entra en courant. « Mais où vas-tu ? » demanda
> Marie. « J'ai cours dans dix minutes, répondit-il, et je ne
> trouve plus mon stylo ». « Tu es impossible ! » fit Marie.
> « Tu l'avais hier soir, ce stylo. Je me souviens très bien.
> Tu ne te rappelles pas ? »

ANSWERS TO EXERCISES

Introduction

Exercise 1
Transcription of the passage.

> She was beginning to get very tired of sitting by her sister
> on the bank and of having nothing to do: once or twice she
> had peeped into the book her sister was reading, but it had
> no pictures or conversations in it, and what is the use of a
> book, she thought, without pictures or conversations?

Exercise 2
Transcription of the passage.

> Cela commençait à la fatiguer de rester assise ainsi à côté
> de sa soeur sur le talus sans avoir rien à faire. Une ou deux
> fois elle avait jeté un coup d'oeil furtif dans le livre que
> lisait sa soeur, mais il ne contenait ni illustrations ni
> conversations et à quoi servait donc un livre, se disait-elle,
> sans illustrations ni conversations ?

I. Syllables and syllabification

Exercise 1
Organise the words of the following sentences into two lists.

List 1 (open syllables): le /lə/, rentraient /ʀɑ̃tʀɛ/, des /de/,
champs /ʃɑ̃/, les /le/, parents /paʀɑ̃/, chat /ʃa/, la /la/,
du /dy/, puit /pɥi/, où /u/, était /etɛ/, occupé /ɔkype/,

PRONOUNCING FRENCH

à /a/, sa /sa/, allons /alɔ̃/, voilà /vwala/, qui /ki/, pardessus /paʀdəsy/, son /sɔ̃/, va /va/, demain /dəmɛ̃/.

List 2 (closed syllables): soir /swaʀ/, comme /kɔm/, ils /il/ trouvent /tʀuv/, sur /syʀ/, margelle /maʀʒɛl/, il /il/, faire /fɛʀ/, toilette /twalɛt/, dirent-ils /diʀtil/, passe /pas/, patte /pat/, oreille /ɔʀɛj/, encore /ɑ̃kɔʀ/, pleuvoir /pløvwaʀ/.

Exercise 2
La/prin/ci/pal(e)/nou/veau/té/so/cial(e)/du/temps/est/l'a/ppa
/ri/tion/du/pro/lé/ta/riat/in/dus/triel//dont/les/con/di/tions/
de/vie/é/taient/in/fi/ni/ment/plus/di/ffi/cil(es)/que/cell(es)/de
/l'ou/vri/er/du/sec/teur/ar/ti/sa/nal/.

2. Stress and rhythm

Exercise 1
Transcription of the passage.

> En effet, le lendemain, la pluie tomba toute la journée.
> Il ne fallait pas penser à aller travailler. Fachés de ne
> pouvoir mettre le nez dehors, les parents étaient de
> mauvaise humeur et peu patients avec leurs deux filles.

Exercise 2
/ɛ̃despɛktakl/
/laspeʒeneʀal/
/ləpœplfʀɑ̃sɛ/
/ɛ̃vastʃɑ̃/
/yntɑ̃pɛtdənɛʒ/
/devizaʒøʀø/
/ʒəsɥifatige/
/mɛsavapa/
/ilfɛbo/
/kəmvulevu/

3. Oral vowels I
([u], [y], [i], [a], [e], [o] and [ø])

Exercise 1

reçut /ʀəsy/, curieux /kyʀjø/, tumeur /tymœʀ/, début /deby/.

Exercise 2

vétérinaire /veteʀinɛʀ/, étude /etyd/, éventuelle /evãtɥɛl/, est /e/, expériences /ɛkspɛʀjãs/, diligentées /diliʒãte/, concernés /kɔ̃sɛʀne/, conséquences /kɔ̃sekãs/, poulet /pule/, familier /familje/, consommé /kɔ̃sɔme/.

Exercise 3

heureux /øʀø/, neveux /nəvø/, peu /pø/, deux /dø/, ennuyeux /ãnɥijø/.

Exercise 4

/la seʀinwaʀ elœvʀdəsezotœʀ sɛʀt mɛzosi dəlekipdədyamɛl ki asylɛ̃pose paʀlakalite dəseʃwa seʀɛgldətʀadyksjɔ̃ epaʀlymuʀdəsetitʀ // sɔ̃sykse vjɛ̃tildəsɔ̃ʀɔmãtismnwaʀ dəsɔ̃nekʀityʀ pʀɔʃdəlapɛ̃tyʀ sinematɔgʀafik udeʀɛv kɛlpɔʀt // ɛletosi lɛ̃desiɲ dynfʀãs kisəʀəkɔ̃stʀɥi esinisi atatɔ̃ esãtʀo ləsavwaʀ omɔdɛl ameʀikɛ̃/

4. Oral vowels 2
([ɛ], [ə], [ɔ], [œ] and [ɑ])

Exercise 1

revenu /ʀəvny/, de /də/, le /lə/, fenêtres /fənɛtʀ/, première /pʀəmjɛʀ/, je /ʒə/, ne /nə/, me /mə/, repartir /ʀəpaʀtiʀ/, regrettant /ʀəgʀetã/.

Exercise 2
heure /œʀ/, soeur /sœʀ/, aveugle /avœgl/,
jeune /jœn/, facteur /faktœʀ/, beurre /bœʀ/.

Exercise 3
1. pot, pots, peau, peaux
2. mot, mots, maux
3. à, a
4. ce, se
5. on, ont

6. près, prêt
7. tôt, taux
8. son, sont
9. au, aux, eau, eaux, haut, hauts
10. dans, dent, dents

Exercise 4
Monsieur Lenoir entra dans la pièce sans se retourner pour voir si sa femme le suivait. C'était un atelier de réparation de moteurs électriques et le sol était couvert de bouts de fils de toutes couleurs. La jeune femme fut étonnée par la vue des entrailles d'appareils ménagers qu'elle connaissait bien et dont elle ne soupçonnait pas la complexité des méchanismes intérieurs. Le chef d'équipe se leva de son établi et s'avança vers Monsieur Lenoir pour lui serrer la main.

Exercise 5
nunetjɔ̃pasyʀ dərɑʒwɛ̃dʀlacot // ʒavɛzɑ̃vwaje
ɛ̃mɛsaʒʀadjo opɔʀ puʀkɔ̃nuzɑ̃vwa ɛ̃batodəsovtaʒ //
levag etɛ de plyzɑ̃plyot elaʃalup pʀənɛlo // nukɔmɑ̃sjɔ̃
aavwaʀpœʀ // ɑ̃kɔʀœʀœkilfasɑ̃kɔʀʒuʀ kʀijapɔl
puʀbʀize ɛ̃silɑ̃s kidəvnɛluʀ // apɛnytilpaʀle kapaʀy
ababɔʀ lavədɛt degaʀdkot dəlilnwaʀ.

5. Nasal vowels

Exercise 1
Léon [ɔ̃], Alain [ɛ̃], Gaston [ɔ̃], Constance [ɔ̃] and [ɑ̃],
Sébastien [ɛ̃], Simon [ɔ̃], Julien [ɛ̃], Henri [ɑ̃].

6. Glide approximants

Exercise 1

Oui [w], puis [ɥ], tuer [ɥ], louer [w], feuille [j], fruit [ɥ],
mouette [w], lier [j], famille [j], ouate [w], oiseau [w],
Louise [w], payer [j], hier [j].

Exercise 2

/sɛtnɥi lavilekalm ilfɛnwaʀ eləvã vjɛ̃dəlwɛst //
lwisɔmnɔl susakwɛt // dãleʀɥel ynjœnfij puʀsɥi
sɔ̃ʃəmɛ̃ sulalyn bʀijãt // ileɥitœʀ // sudɛ̃ ləpɔʀtaj
suvʀ // lwitãlɔʀej // ilɛsɛdãtãdʀ lafijãtʀe dãlakuʀ /

7. The consonants /p/, /t/, /k/ and /b/, /d/, /g/

Exercise 1

1. /sekãkilaʀiv/
2. /sekɔmãkɛlfɛsa/
3. /kiɛskilavy/
4. /sekɔ̃bjɛ̃səlivʀ/

Exercise 2

1. /sepapakiafɛsɛtpulopo/
2. /pɔlapʀimɔ̃pɔʀtmɔnɛ/
3. /patʀisja apɔʀte səpanje/
4. /sepjɛʀkjapejelpo/

Exercise 3

1. /tyvødyte/
2. /tyvøyntaʀtin/
3. /tyvødetost/
4. /tyvøyntʀãʃdətɔm/

Exercise 4

1. /bʀiʒit labalɛje avɛkynbʀãʃ/
2. /labɛlbaʀbaʀa ebʀyn/
3. /blãʃ səbʀɔs ledã/
4. /bɛʀnaʀ ebʀav ebɔ̃/

8. The consonants R and l

Exercise 2

1. Demain, elle garera sa voiture.
2. Il arrivera demain soir.
3. Marie pourra partir demain.
4. Je rirai demain.
5. Hélène rentrera demain.
6. Pierre reviendra demain.
7. Je verrai ce film demain après-midi.
8. Elle finira de travailler demain.

9. Liaisons

Exercise 1

/Sɛtnɥitulvilaʒesulalyn/ilʒɛl/ileɥitœR/opRəmjɛRetaʒle
bɔ̃zami/sdizɔRvwaR/setɔ̃nanivɛRsɛRdmɛ̃pɔl/ɔ̃feynfɛt/ʃe
pjɛRɛRəne/sesɛ̃patikʃezø/mesɑ̃lezotRzamibjɛ̃ɑ̃tɑ̃dy/nub
lijepamaRi/ɛlaseptitzabityd/leʒɑ̃aRivRɔ̃taRʒkRwa/ilsRɔ̃t
epɥizeapRɛlœRtRavaj/

Exercise 2

(a) *optional liaisons*

se disant au revoir
seront épuisés

(b) *obligatory liaisons*

premier étage /pRəmjɛRɛtaʒ/
bons amis /bɔ̃z a mi/
ton anniversaire /tɔ̃naivɛRsɛR/
chez eux /ʃezø/
les autres amis /lezotRəzami/
bien entendu /bjɛ̃nɑ̃tɑ̃dy/
petites habitudes /pətitzabitud/

10 Rhythm and intonation

Exercise 1

/pɔlɑ̃tʀa ɑ̃kuʀɑ̃ // mɛ uvaty / dəmɑ̃damaʀi //
jɛkuʀdɑ̃diminyt /ʀepɔ̃ditil / ejəntʀuvply mɔ̃stilo //
tyeɛ̃posibl / fimaʀi // tylavɛjɛʀswaʀ səstilo /
ʒəməsuvjɛ̃tʀɛbjɛ̃ / tyntəʀapɛlpa /

Further reading

Abercrombie, D. (1991) *Fifty Years in Phonetics*. Edinburgh: Edinburgh University Press.

Argod-Dutard, F. (1996) *Eléments de phonétique appliquée*, Paris: Armand Colin

Bongaerts, T., C. van Summeren, B. Planken, and E. Schils (1997) 'Age and ultimate attainment in the pronunciation of a foreign language', *Studies in Second Language Acquisition*, 19: 447–65.

Callamand, M. (1981) *Méthodologie de l'enseignement de la prononciation: organisation de la matière phonique de français et correction phonétique*. Paris: CLE International.

Clark, J. and C. Yallop (1990) *An Introduction to Phonetics and Phonology*. Cambridge, MA: Blackwell.

Crystal, D. (1991) *A Dictionary of Linguistics and Phonetics*. Cambridge, MA: Blackwell.

Crystal, D. (1995) *The Cambridge Encyclopedia of the English Language*. Cambridge: Cambridge University Press.

Delattre, P. (1965) *Comparing the Phonetic Features of French, English, German and Spanish*. Heidelberg: Julius Groos.

Gimson, A. (1980) *An Introduction to the Pronunciation of English*. London: Edward Arnold.

Kenworthy, J. (2000) *The Pronunciation of English*, London: Arnold

Kriedler, C. W. (1997) *Describing Spoken English: An Introduction*. London: Routledge.

Ladefoged, P. (1993) *A Course in Phonetics*, 3rd edn. Fort Worth, TX: Harcourt Brace Jovanovich.

Ladefoged, P. and I. Maddiesen (1996) *The Sounds of the World's Languages*. Oxford: Blackwell.

Léon, P. R. (1968) (ed.), *Recherches sur la structure phonique du français canadien*. Montreal: Didier.

Léon, P. R. (1966) *Prononciation du français standard*. Montreal: Didier.

Mougeon, R. and E. Beniak (1989) *Le francais canadien parle hors Quebec*. Quebec: Presses de l'Université Laval.

Picard, M. (1987) *An Introduction to the Comparative Phonetics of English and French in North America*. Amsterdam: John Benjamins.

Price, G. (1991) *An Introduction to French Pronunciation*, Oxford: Blackwell.

Thomas, A. (1987) *La variation phonétique: cas du franco-ontarien*. Montreal: Didier.

Tranel, B. (1987) *The Sounds of French*. Cambridge: Cambridge University Press.

Trask, R.L. (1996) *A Dictionary of Linguistics and Phonetics*. London and New York: Routledge.

Unwin, E. E. (2001) *An Introductory Course in French Phonetics*. London: Blackie.

Walter, H. (1976) *La dynamique des phonèmes dans le lexique français contemporain*. Paris: France Expansion.

Walter, H. (1977) *La phonologie du français*, Paris: Presses Universitaires de France.

Walter, H. (1982) *Enquête phonologique et variétés régionales du français*. Paris: Presses Universitaires de France.

Wolfram, W. and N. Schilling-Estes (1998) *American English*. Oxford: Blackwell.

Appendix: IPA phonetic symbols

French		English		French		English	
VOWELS		VOWELS		CONSONANTS		CONSONANTS	
[ə]	le	[ə]	ago	[p]	pont	[p]	pen
[a]	plat	[æ]	hat	[t]	ton	[t]	tea
[ɑ]	pâte	[ɑ:]	arm	[k]	cou	[k]	cat
[ɑ̃]	vent	[e]	ten	[b]	bon	[b]	bad
[e]	né	[ɜ]	fur	[d]	don	[d]	did
[ɛ]	lait	[ɪ]	sit	[g]	goût	[g]	got
[ɛ̃]	vin	[i:]	see	[f]	fou	[f]	fall
[i]	lit	[ɔ:]	saw	[s]	sous	[s]	so
[ɔ]	mort	[ɒ]	got	[ʃ]	chou	[ʃ]	she
[o]	beau	[ʊ]	put	[v]	vous	[v]	voice
[ɔ̃]	bon	[u:]	too	[z]	zéro	[z]	zoo
[ø]	peu	[ʌ]	cup	[ʒ]	je	[ʒ]	vision
[œ]	peur			[l]	lent	[l]	lane
[œ̃]	brun			[ʀ]	raie	[r]	red
[u]	cou	DIPHTHONGS		[m]	mon	[m]	man
[y]	vu			[n]	non	[n]	no
		[əʊ]	home	[ɲ]	vigne	[ŋ]	sing
		[aɪ]	five	[ŋ]	dancing	[w]	wet
SEMI-VOWELS		[aʊ]	now			[tʃ]	chin
		[eə]	hair			[j]	yes
[j]	hier, yeux	[ɛɪ]	page			[dʒ]	June
[w]	oui, noix	[ɪə]	near			[θ]	thin
[ɥ]	huile, lui	[ɔɪ]	join			[ð]	then
		[ʊə]	pure			[h]	how

Index

79